What Is Window Dressing and Why It Matters?

Window dressing, also known as **visual merchandising**, is the strategic arrangement of products, props, and decorative elements in a shop window or store interior to attract customers and enhance their shopping experience. It's not just an aesthetic choice—it's a business strategy.

In today's world, where online shopping is on the rise, **physical stores need to offer something extra**—a reason for customers to stop, step inside, and experience the brand. A well-designe͟ ͟ ͟display can:

- **Increase foot traffic** by drawing people

- **Create brand identity** and tell a story

- **Encourage impulse purchases** by sparking ͟ ͟

- **Showcase new arrivals or promotions** in an eye-catching way

- **Engage emotions** and make shopping a memorable experience

For example, luxury brands use **elegance and minimalism** to communicate exclusivity, while toy stores create **colorful and playful displays** to appeal to children and their parents. Supermarkets place **freshly baked goods near the entrance** because the smell triggers hunger, leading to more purchases. Everything is intentional.

Window dressing is the **first handshake between a store and its potential customers**—and first impressions count.

The Impact of Visual Merchandising on Sales

A stunning display isn't just about looking good—it has a direct impact on sales. Research has shown that **80% of sensory information comes from sight**, and **more than half of purchase decisions are made in-store**. This means that what a customer sees and experiences plays a huge role in their buying behavior.

Some key ways visual merchandising boosts sales:

1. Capturing Attention & Driving Footfall

In a crowded shopping district, your store is competing with dozens—if not hundreds—of others. A creative window display acts like a magnet, drawing people in.

- A **bold color scheme** can make your store stand out from a distance.

- Strategic **lighting** can highlight key products and create mood.

- **Motion displays** (such as rotating mannequins or digital screens) attract the eye instantly.

2. Influencing Customer Behavior

Once inside, customers are subtly guided by store layouts and visual cues. Well-placed signage, lighting, and product arrangements **direct attention to high-margin items** or encourage impulse buys.

Eye-level displays increase product visibility and sales.
Limited-time offers with strong visuals create urgency.
Storytelling displays make products feel more personal and desirable.

Beginners Guide To Window Dressing

Introduction

Imagine walking down a bustling high street or through a shopping mall. Among the sea of stores, one window display catches your eye. Maybe it's a beautifully curated scene that tells a story, an unexpected pop of color, or a clever use of lighting that makes a product irresistible. Without realizing it, you slow down, take a closer look, and before you know it—you're stepping inside.

This is the magic of **window dressing** and **visual merchandising**. It's not just about making a storefront look pretty; it's about **capturing attention, evoking emotions, and ultimately driving sales**. A well-designed shop display acts as a silent salesperson, drawing people in, creating desire, and converting passersby into paying customers.

In this guide, we'll explore the art and psychology of window dressing and shop displays. Whether you're a business owner, a designer, or someone fascinated by the world of retail, this book will equip you with the tools, techniques, and insights needed to create compelling displays that truly work.

3. Creating a Memorable Experience

A visually stunning display isn't just about selling products—it's about selling an experience. Customers are more likely to return and recommend stores that engage them emotionally.

- Think of the magical holiday window displays in New York, Paris, or London—people flock to see them, take photos, and share them on social media.

- Interactive elements, such as touchscreen catalogs or AR experiences, enhance engagement.

- A well-thought-out store ambiance (lighting, music, scent) turns shopping into a sensory journey.

By mastering visual merchandising, you're **not just decorating a store—you're shaping how people shop, feel, and spend.**

Understanding Consumer Psychology in Retail

Behind every successful shop display lies a deep understanding of **how customers think and behave**. Human psychology plays a crucial role in determining what attracts shoppers, how they make decisions, and what drives them to buy.

1. The Power of First Impressions

People form first impressions within **7 seconds**, and **window displays are often the first touchpoint**. If a display sparks interest, curiosity, or an emotional reaction, the likelihood of a customer stepping inside increases.

- **Warm colors like red, orange, and yellow** create excitement and urgency.

- **Cool colors like blue and green** evoke trust and relaxation.

- **Minimalist displays suggest luxury and exclusivity,** while busy, cluttered ones can feel overwhelming.

2. The Role of Emotion in Shopping

Shopping is not just a rational process—it's emotional. **People buy based on feelings and justify with logic.**

- **Nostalgic displays** (vintage aesthetics, holiday themes) create a sentimental connection.

- **Luxury brands use scarcity and exclusivity** (e.g., "limited edition" labels) to drive demand.

- **Interactive elements** (e.g., "Try Me" stations, digital mirrors) make shopping fun and engaging.

3. The Psychology of Product Placement

How products are positioned affects what customers buy.

- **Best-selling items should be at eye level**—this is the "buy zone."

- **Impulse-buy products** (small, affordable items) should be placed near checkout counters.

- **Grouping products together** (e.g., shoes next to handbags) encourages cross-selling.

By using psychological triggers effectively, you can turn window shoppers into loyal customers.

Tools and Materials You'll Need

Creating a show-stopping display doesn't require a massive budget, but it does require the **right tools and materials**. Here's a basic list to get you started:

Essential Tools

- **Mannequins or display stands** – Perfect for showcasing clothing and accessories.

- **Lighting equipment** – Spotlights, LED strips, and colored lights enhance visibility.

- **Adhesives & fasteners** – Tape, Velcro, and hooks for securing elements.

- **Signage & lettering** – Custom signage for promotions and branding.

- **Props & backdrops** – Fabric, wood, or foam boards to set the scene.

Materials for Creative Displays

- **Acrylic or glass panels** – For sleek, modern designs.

- **Paper & cardboard** – Cost-effective for DIY elements.

- **Fake plants, flowers, or artificial snow** – Adds texture and realism.

- **Mirrors** – Creates depth and an illusion of a larger space.

- **Screens or projectors** – Digital elements for modern displays.

Mastering window dressing is both an **art and a science**. By understanding **visual principles, consumer psychology, and merchandising techniques**, you can create **displays that not only look stunning but also drive real business results**.

The Psychology Behind Effective Displays

Have you ever walked past a store and felt an irresistible urge to stop and stare at the window display? Maybe it was a striking color combination, a perfectly placed spotlight, or a story being told that spoke to you on an emotional level. This is no accident—**it's psychology at work**.

Window displays are **silent salespeople**. They don't speak, but they communicate. They tell stories, evoke emotions, and **guide customer behavior** in ways that most people don't even realize. A great display is not just about aesthetics; it's about **understanding the human mind** and using that knowledge to create a compelling experience that **attracts, engages, and converts passersby into paying customers**.

The Science of First Impressions

You have **seven seconds** to make an impression. That's all.

In those few moments, a potential customer's brain makes a **snap judgment** about your store. Is it worth their time? Does it appeal to them? Is it high-end or budget-friendly? Does it feel exciting, inviting, or forgettable?

What Makes a First Impression Stick?

* **Contrast & Boldness** – Displays that use contrast (dark vs. light, bold colors, or unexpected elements) grab attention faster.
* **Symmetry & Balance** – People naturally prefer **organized, symmetrical** displays over chaotic ones.
* **Movement & Depth** – Elements that move (rotating platforms, digital screens) or create depth (layering objects) keep the eye engaged.
* **Lighting & Focus** – Brightly lit, well-focused displays create a feeling of importance, directing attention to key areas.

The Role of Color Psychology in Retail

Color is more than just decoration—it's a trigger for emotion and behavior. Brands spend millions choosing the right colors for their logos, packaging, and advertising because they know different shades **affect how people feel and act**.

Let's break down the psychological effects of different colors in shop displays:

1. Warm Colors (Red, Orange, Yellow) – Energy & Urgency

These colors create a sense of **excitement, action, and impulse buying**.
■ **Red** – Stimulates appetite (why do you think McDonald's and Coca-Cola use it?), increases heart rate, and creates urgency (SALE signs).
■ **Orange** – Encourages friendliness and affordability (great for discount stores).
■ **Yellow** – Grabs attention and creates happiness (often used in children's stores).

2. Cool Colors (Blue, Green, Purple) – Trust & Calmness

These colors **evoke trust, relaxation, and sophistication**.
■ **Blue** – Associated with trust and professionalism (why banks and tech companies love it).
■ **Green** – Represents health and nature (perfect for organic brands).
■ **Purple** – Suggests luxury and creativity (commonly used for beauty and high-end products).

3. Neutral Colors (Black, White, Gray, Brown) – Elegance & Minimalism

These colors convey **sophistication and timelessness**.
■ **Black & White** – Often used in high-end retail to suggest luxury and exclusivity.
■ **Gray & Brown** – Provide a natural, down-to-earth feel, often used in eco-conscious branding.

💡 **Pro Tip:** Ever notice why high-end jewelry stores use **black backgrounds**? It makes diamonds and gold pop, creating **contrast and perceived value**.

How Lighting Affects Mood and Buyer Decisions

Lighting isn't just about visibility—it's about **creating an emotional atmosphere**. The right lighting can make a store feel **warm and inviting or cool and exclusive**, and it **guides shoppers toward specific products**.

Types of Lighting & Their Effects:

* **Bright, White Light (Cool-Toned LED)** – Used in **tech stores, clinics, and supermarkets** to create a clean, efficient, and focused environment.
* **Soft, Warm Light (Yellow-Hued Bulbs)** – Common in **boutiques, cafes, and bookstores** to create comfort and relaxation.
* **Spotlights & Accent Lighting** – Used to highlight **premium products, jewelry, or high-end fashion**—making them appear more valuable.
* **Neon or Colored Lighting** – Adds a **trendy, playful** vibe (popular in sneaker stores and pop culture brands).
* **Motion-Activated or Interactive Lighting** – Engages customers and encourages them to stay longer (used in high-tech and experience-based retail).

💡 **Pro Tip:** Experiment with lighting by changing **shadows and brightness**. Even a small shift in lighting can **change how luxurious or budget-friendly** a product looks.

Storytelling Through Window Displays

Humans love stories. They make us feel something. A good window display isn't just a collection of products—it's a **visual narrative** that **immerses the shopper in an experience**.

How to Use Storytelling in Your Displays:

+ **Create a Theme** – A great display has a clear **concept or mood** (e.g., a Parisian café scene for a fashion brand or a winter wonderland for a holiday sale).
+ **Use Props & Scenery** – Go beyond mannequins and hangers—add **props that enhance the story** (e.g., a travel-themed display might include vintage suitcases and maps).
+ **Evoke Emotion** – Ask yourself: **How do I want people to feel?** Excited? Nostalgic? Inspired?
+ **Keep It Cohesive** – Everything in your display should support the story—the color scheme, props, lighting, and even the fonts used in signage.

🔦 **Pro Tip:** If your display was a **still frame in a movie**, would it **tell a story** without words? If not, refine your design.

The Power of Minimalism vs. Clutter

When it comes to **display design**, more isn't always better.

A cluttered display overwhelms the eye and **confuses shoppers**, while a well-balanced, minimalistic setup draws focus to **what truly matters**.

Why Minimalism Works:

■ **Luxury Appeal** – High-end brands use **empty space and a few key pieces** to create a sense of exclusivity.

■ **Easier Decision-Making** – When shoppers aren't bombarded with too many choices, they make **quicker purchasing decisions**.

■ **Higher Perceived Value** – A sparse display **elevates the importance** of the featured products.

When Clutter Works:

■ **For Discount or Budget Stores** – A "treasure hunt" feeling encourages browsing.

■ **For Seasonal Promotions** – Holiday displays packed with festive elements create excitement.

■ **For Interactive Experiences** – If a display encourages **touching and playing** with items, a busy setup can be engaging.

💡 **Pro Tip:** Follow the **"Rule of Three"**—group items in sets of **three or five** rather than crowding them. It keeps the display **visually balanced and pleasing**.

The best window displays don't just look beautiful—they **influence behavior, trigger emotions, and create unforgettable experiences**. By mastering the psychology of **first impressions, color, lighting, storytelling, and display balance**, you can turn window shoppers into loyal customers.

Principles of Effective Window Dressing

Window displays are more than just an arrangement of products—they're a **silent invitation** to customers, a story told through design, and a powerful tool to **boost foot traffic and sales**. The most successful displays don't happen by chance; they follow key **design principles** that make them visually appealing and psychologically engaging.

Balance, Symmetry, and Visual Weight

Ever seen a display that just *feels right*? That's because of **balance**. Our brains naturally crave **harmony**, and when a window display is well-balanced, it looks professional, intentional, and **pleasing to the eye**.

Types of Balance in Display Design:

* **Symmetrical Balance** – This is when both sides of the display are **mirror images** of each other. It creates a sense of **stability, luxury, and formality**. High-end brands often use this approach because it suggests **elegance and order**.
  Example: A jewelry store with two identical mannequins on either side of a central product display.

* **Asymmetrical Balance** – Here, different elements are placed to **create balance without perfect symmetry**. This makes the display feel **dynamic and modern**.
  Example: A clothing boutique showcasing a large mannequin on one side, balanced by a smaller table display on the other.

* **Radial Balance** – All elements revolve around a **central focal point**, guiding the eye to the most important part of the display.

Example: A circular display with shoes arranged around a central, illuminated handbag.

Understanding Visual Weight

Not all objects in a display carry the same "weight." **Larger, brighter, or more colorful elements feel heavier**, so they naturally draw the eye. You can balance this by placing **smaller, darker, or less intense elements strategically** around the display.

💡 **Pro Tip:** Step back and **squint at your display**. If one side feels "heavier" than the other, adjust until the visual weight feels evenly distributed.

Focal Points: Drawing the Eye to Key Products

Your display has **three seconds** to grab attention. If the eye doesn't know *where* to look, people will **glance and move on**. That's why every display needs a **clear focal point**—a visual "anchor" that immediately draws attention.

How to Create a Strong Focal Point:

■ **Use Size to Your Advantage** – The largest item in your display should be your focal point.

■ **Make It Stand Out with Color** – A bold color contrast will naturally pull the viewer's attention.

■ **Lighting is Everything** – Spotlighting a product **instantly increases its importance**.

■ **Position It at Eye Level** – People look straight ahead first, so place your most important product where it will be seen.

🔦 **Pro Tip:** Avoid **focal point confusion**. If there are **too many competing elements**, customers won't know where to look. Keep it simple!

Layering and Depth for Visual Interest

A great window display isn't **flat**—it has **depth, movement, and dimension**. Think of it like **a stage set** rather than a poster.

How to Create Depth in Your Display:

* **Use Multiple Layers** – Instead of placing everything in a straight line, create a **foreground, middle ground, and background**.
* **Vary Heights & Angles** – Items placed at **different heights and angles** create a more **dynamic** look.
* **Incorporate Reflections & Shadows** – Mirrors and transparent elements add **dimension** and keep the display from looking two-dimensional.
* **Utilize Props for Texture** – Fabric drapes, wooden crates, or metal structures create layers **without overpowering** the main products.

Example of Layering in Action:

Imagine a holiday display for a **luxury perfume brand**:

✦ **Foreground:** A delicate sheer curtain partially covering the window, drawing curiosity.

✦ **Middle ground:** The featured perfumes placed on **elevated glass stands** at different heights.

✦ **Background:** A softly lit **Parisian skyline print**, adding a dreamy atmosphere.

🔦 **Pro Tip:** Depth **keeps customers engaged longer**—the longer they look, the more likely they are to enter the store.

Motion and Interactive Displays

What if your display **moved**? What if customers could **interact** with it? Adding motion or **an interactive element** can turn a passive display into a **memorable experience**.

How Motion Captures Attention:

- **Rotating Displays** – Slowly moving platforms highlight products from every angle.
- **Kinetic Installations** – Think of gently swaying fabric, floating balloons, or moving gears.
- **Digital Screens** – A short looping video showcasing how a product is used **adds storytelling**.
- **Automated Lighting Changes** – A display that shifts from warm morning tones to cooler evening hues keeps it **dynamic and engaging**.

Interactive Displays That Invite Engagement:

- **Touchscreens** – Let customers explore product variations or learn about features with a simple tap.
- **Try-Me Stations** – If possible, allow customers to **smell, touch, or test** products.
- **Photo-Worthy Moments** – A unique, Instagrammable setup encourages **social media shares**, increasing brand exposure.
- **Augmented Reality (AR) Features** – QR codes linked to **virtual try-ons** or product demonstrations add a **tech-forward edge**.

Example of an Interactive Display in Action:

A **sports store** promoting running shoes could have a **mini treadmill in the window**, where passersby can step on and see a **digital analysis of their running form**, leading them to the perfect shoe recommendation.

💡 **Pro Tip: Movement attracts the eye faster than still images**. Even small motion effects, like twinkling fairy lights or gently swaying decorations, can make a display more **magnetic**.

Mastering window dressing isn't just about **making things look pretty**—it's about understanding how to **guide the viewer's eye, create balance, add depth, and engage the senses**. By applying these principles, your displays will **not only capture attention but also convert passersby into customers**.

✦ **Balance & Symmetry** create a harmonious, polished look.
✦ **Focal Points** ensure the most important products stand out.
✦ **Layering & Depth** add richness and keep the eye engaged.
✦ **Motion & Interaction** make displays **memorable and dynamic**.

Designing Your Shop Window: Turning Passersby into Customers

Your shop window is **your brand's handshake**—the first impression that can **stop people in their tracks** or let them walk by unnoticed. A well-designed display isn't just about showcasing products; it's about **creating an experience** that connects with customers emotionally and makes them want to step inside.

Choosing a Theme and Concept

Every great window display starts with a **strong concept**. Instead of randomly arranging products, think of your window as a **mini-stage** where you're telling a story.

How to Pick the Right Theme:

■ **Align with Your Brand** – A high-end boutique should have a different aesthetic than a quirky vintage store. Make sure your theme reflects your store's **personality and values**.

■ **Highlight Your Best-Selling or Newest Products** – What do you want customers to notice **first**?

■ **Think About Your Target Audience** – Are they drawn to luxury? Fun and playfulness? Minimalism?

■ **Create an Emotional Connection** – The best displays evoke **joy, nostalgia, curiosity, or excitement**.

Popular Window Display Themes:

🌿 **Nature & Sustainability** – Wooden crates, plants, and earthy tones to promote eco-friendly products.

🎭 **Theatrical & Dramatic** – A bold, artistic showcase with extravagant lighting and props.

📕 **Storybook Magic** – Fairy tale or fantasy elements that transport viewers into another world.

🛠️ **Behind-the-Scenes** – A raw, "work in progress" display featuring mannequins being "styled" or products mid-assembly.

💡 **Pro Tip:** When in doubt, ask: *What emotion do I want people to feel when they see this display?* If you can answer that, you're on the right track.

Seasonal and Trend-Based Displays

Keeping your display **fresh** is crucial. A stagnant window tells customers, "Nothing new here!" Meanwhile, a **seasonal or trend-based** window creates urgency—people know they need to act fast before the moment passes.

Seasonal Displays That Convert:

🌲 **Winter Holidays** – Think **warm lights, cozy textures, and festive colors** to create a magical, inviting scene.

🌸 **Spring Awakening** – Bright florals, pastel tones, and airy fabrics signal renewal and freshness.

☀️ **Summer Fun** – Beach vibes, vacation themes, and vibrant colors create an **energetic, carefree mood**.

🍂 **Autumn Coziness** – Warm oranges, wood textures, and rustic elements make shoppers crave **comfort and nostalgia**.

Trend-Based Displays:

Following trends keeps your store **relevant and exciting**. Trends can come from:

📺 **Pop Culture** – TV shows, movies, and viral internet trends.

🎨 **Fashion and Interior Design** – Pantone's Color of the Year or trending patterns like **bold geometric prints or minimalistic neutrals**.

📱 **Social Media** – TikTok, Instagram, and Pinterest can reveal **what's hot right now**.

⚫ **Cultural Moments** – Themed displays for **local events, festivals, or sports championships** can draw in crowds.

💡 **Pro Tip:** Always have a **calendar** with upcoming events, holidays, and trends so you can plan your window changes **ahead of time**.

Creating a Narrative with Props and Signage

A great window **doesn't just show products—it tells a story**. And stories are what make people stop, look, and engage.

How to Use Props Effectively:

* **Props should complement, not overpower** – They add context, but your **product remains the star**.
* **Use unexpected elements** – A bookstore could create a display where **pages of books "fly" through the air**.
* **Create depth with layers** – Instead of a flat display, add **foreground, midground, and background elements**.

Signage That Speaks to Your Customers:

Keep It Short & Impactful – People only have a few seconds to read, so **make it count**.

Make It Visually Appealing – Handwritten chalkboards, neon signs, or bold typography catch the eye.

Call to Action (CTA) – "Limited Time Only," "New Collection Inside," or "Try It Today" can **increase urgency and foot traffic**.

Pro Tip: Use **clever wordplay** to make your display more memorable. A bakery could have a sign that says, "Donut pass us by!"

Digital Integration: Screens, QR Codes, and Augmented Reality

Technology is changing the **retail game**, and digital integration can take your window display **to the next level**.

Screens and Video Displays

📺 **Loop product demonstrations** – A video showing a skincare product's **before-and-after results**.

🎥 **Behind-the-scenes footage** – Show how your products are made to add an **authentic, handmade feel**.

🛍️ **Showcase customer testimonials** – A short clip of happy customers talking about why they love your brand.

QR Codes for Instant Engagement

🔗 **Direct to Online Shopping** – Customers can scan to **shop the look instantly**.

📟 **Exclusive Offers & Discounts** – A QR code can give them a **secret promo code** to use in-store.

📱 **Augmented Reality (AR) Features** – Customers can scan a QR code to see **virtual product try-ons, 3D animations, or interactive experiences**.

Augmented Reality: The Future of Window Displays

AR can turn **passive viewers into engaged customers**. Imagine:

👗 **A clothing store where passersby can scan a QR code to "try on" outfits digitally**.

🖼️ **An art gallery display where scanning a QR code brings paintings to life**.

🔍 **A toy store where a digital animation makes action figures "move" in the display**.

💡 **Pro Tip:** Digital elements should **enhance** your display, not replace its core storytelling. Keep the **physical and digital** working together for the best results.

Designing a shop window isn't just about **making it look good**—it's about making people **feel something** and compelling them to take action.

✨ **A strong theme** makes your display cohesive and engaging.
✨ **Seasonal and trend-based updates** keep your window fresh and exciting.
✨ **Props and signage** add storytelling and personality.
✨ **Digital tools like QR codes and AR** create interactive experiences that drive conversions.

By combining **creativity, psychology, and innovation**, you can turn your shop window into **your most powerful sales tool**—one that not only grabs attention but **transforms passersby into loyal customers**.

Understanding Your Target Audience: The Key to Creating Irresistible Displays

A beautifully designed window display means nothing if it doesn't **speak to the right people**. Understanding your target audience is **the secret ingredient** that transforms an ordinary display into one that **connects, engages, and sells**.

Why? Because different shoppers **think, feel, and buy differently**. A display that works for a high-end luxury boutique won't work for a quirky, budget-friendly gift shop. You need to **understand who's walking by** and what makes them stop, look, and step inside.

Shopper Demographics and Their Behaviors

Before designing a display, ask yourself:
- 🛍 *Who are my customers?*
- ⬤ *What do they care about?*
- 🪓 *How do they make buying decisions?*

Different demographics respond to **different styles, colors, and messages**. Here's how to appeal to the **four major types of shoppers**:

1 The Impulse Buyer (Spontaneous & Emotional)

🔥 **What drives them?** Excitement, urgency, and FOMO (Fear of Missing Out).
👀 **What works?**
🟥 **Bright colors & bold headlines** – "LIMITED EDITION" or "ONLY 5 LEFT!"

■ **Engaging visuals & interactive elements** – Motion-based displays or AR features.

■ **Trendy or seasonal themes** – Tap into what's hot right now!

🛒 *Example:* A fashion store can showcase a mannequin wearing the "look of the season" with a sign that says, *"As Seen on Influencers – Shop the Trend Inside!"*

2 The Practical Shopper (Logical & Budget-Conscious)

● **What drives them?** Value, functionality, and cost-effectiveness.

●● **What works?**

■ **Clear, informative signage** – "Best Value" or "Smart Buy" labels.

■ **Organized and clutter-free displays** – Too much choice can overwhelm them.

■ **Comparison elements** – "Why this product is better" infographics.

🛒 *Example:* A home appliance store could highlight an energy-efficient washing machine with a sign saying, *"Save £100 a year on energy bills – See How Inside!"*

3 The Luxury Shopper (Status & Exclusivity Focused)

◆ **What drives them?** Prestige, quality, and exclusivity.

●● **What works?**

■ **Minimalist, high-end aesthetics** – Think luxury boutique, not bargain bin.

■ **Spotlighting key pieces** – Less is more. Make the display **feel exclusive**.

■ **Premium materials & soft lighting** – Velvet, gold accents, and warm lights enhance luxury.

🛒 *Example:* A jewelry store could use a simple, elegant window with a **single spotlight on a diamond ring**, with text saying, *"A Statement Piece for Those Who Expect the Best."*

4 The Experience-Seeker (Social & Lifestyle-Focused)

🌟 **What drives them?** Experiences, storytelling, and social sharing.

👀 **What works?**

▪ **Interactive displays** – Touchscreens, AR mirrors, or gamified elements.

▪ **Instagrammable setups** – Fun, unique backgrounds people want to take photos with.

▪ **Story-driven themes** – Turn shopping into an **immersive experience**.

🛒 *Example:* A bookstore could have a **Harry Potter-themed window** where visitors can *wave their hands* to reveal hidden text using smart lighting.

💡 **Pro Tip:** Most shoppers don't fit neatly into one category, so combining elements can make your display even **more powerful**.

Emotional Triggers That Drive Purchases

People don't just buy products—they buy **feelings, solutions, and identities**. Understanding **what emotions** drive purchases can help you design displays that **connect deeply** with customers.

◆ The Fear of Missing Out (FOMO)

👉 Works well for **limited-edition** or seasonal items.
⬤ Use words like **"Only a few left!"** or **"Exclusive Collection"** to create urgency.

◆ The Comfort & Nostalgia Effect

👉 Works well for **seasonal displays** (winter coziness, summer memories).
💥 Use **warm lighting, vintage elements, and familiar scents** (candles, pine) to evoke comfort.

◆ The Aspiration Effect (Identity & Status)

👉 Works well for **luxury and fashion brands**.
👑 Use **words like "Elevate Your Style" or "For Those Who Expect the Best."**

◆ The Social Proof Trigger

👉 Works well when people **see others engaging**.
⭐ Showcase **best-sellers**, influencer endorsements, or user-generated content in your display.

🍾 **Pro Tip:** Think about the **emotional story** behind your products. What feeling does someone get when they buy it? That's what you need to showcase.

How to Adapt Your Display for Different Audiences

Your **shop's location, customer base, and industry** will shape the way you design your window. Here's how to tailor your display **based on different audiences**:

◼ High-Street Shoppers (Fast-Paced, Trend-Driven)

✔ **Quick, eye-catching visuals** – They only have a few seconds to notice you.
✔ **Bold and engaging signage** – "NEW IN STORE – DON'T MISS OUT!"
✔ **Lifestyle-focused themes** – Show them **how your product fits into their daily life**.

🛒 *Example:* A sneaker store on a busy street might display sneakers **floating mid-air with a neon sign** saying, *"Run Faster. Jump Higher. Just Do It."*

🐾 Suburban Shoppers (Family-Oriented, Budget-Conscious)

✔ **Practical and clear messaging** – Focus on savings and functionality.
✔ **Warm, welcoming aesthetics** – Soft lighting, friendly signage.
✔ **Seasonal relevance** – Christmas, Back-to-School, or Family Weekend deals.

🛒 *Example:* A toy store in a suburban mall could have a **"Family Fun Night" display** featuring board games, with a sign saying, *"Unplug & Play – Family Game Night Essentials Inside!"*

🧢 Students & Young Adults (Trendy, Digital-Native, Experience-Driven)

✔️ **Tech-integrated elements** – QR codes, social media challenges.
✔️ **Pop culture tie-ins** – References to movies, TV shows, or viral trends.
✔️ **Photo-worthy displays** – A **fun, interactive setup** they'll want to share online.

📝 *Example:* A cosmetics store could create a **TikTok-inspired "Glow-Up Station"**, where customers scan a QR code to see a **before-and-after makeup transformation**.

Know Your Shopper, Win More Sales

A powerful window display isn't just about **looking good**—it's about **understanding who your customers are and what makes them tick.**

- **Identify your key customer types** – Are they impulse buyers, luxury shoppers, or practical budget-seekers?
- **Trigger emotions that drive action** – FOMO, nostalgia, status, and social proof are powerful motivators.
- **Adapt to different audiences** – A high-street display needs a different approach than a suburban boutique.

Practical Steps to Setting Up a Display That Turns Heads and Drives Sales

A **well-executed shop window** is more than just a pretty arrangement of products—it's a **strategic marketing tool** that can **stop people in their tracks, spark curiosity, and drive them through your doors**. But how do you go from an empty window to an eye-catching display that works?

---

1 Planning and Sketching Your Layout: The Blueprint for Success

Before you start **moving mannequins and stacking props**, take a step back and **plan your design on paper (or digitally)**. A well-thought-out layout will help ensure **balance, flow, and impact**.

◆ Start with a Concept

Ask yourself:
🛍️ *What's the main message I want to convey?* (Luxury, fun, urgency, exclusivity?)
🌐 *What colors and themes match the season or product line?*
👀 *What's the best way to capture attention in three seconds or less?*

👉 Example: If you're setting up a **winter holiday display**, your concept might be *"A Cozy Winter Wonderland"* with warm lighting, soft textures, and festive elements.

◆ Sketch It Out

You don't need to be an artist—just a **basic sketch** will help you visualize:

■ **Where each product will go** (front, center, sides, elevated positions).

■ **What fixtures, mannequins, or props you'll need**.

■ **How customers will view it from different angles**.

💡 **Pro Tip:** Use grid paper or digital design tools like **Canva or SketchUp** to create your layout.

---

2 Selecting the Right Products to Feature: Less is More

Not every product in your store needs to be in the window. **Choose wisely** to create **focus and desire**.

◆ How to Pick the Best Products

✔ **Bestsellers & new arrivals** – Highlight what's trending or fresh.

✔ **Seasonally relevant items** – Adapt for holidays, weather, or cultural events.

✔ **High-margin products** – Promote items that bring in the best profit.

✔ **Complementary products** – Show a complete look or solution (e.g., a full outfit instead of just a jacket).

👉 Example: A clothing store featuring **spring fashion** might display a **mannequin in a light pastel outfit**, with matching shoes and accessories nearby, rather than cluttering the space with **dozens of unrelated items**.

💡 **Pro Tip:** Keep **product variety limited**—too many items create **visual chaos**. The best displays have **a clear focal point**.

---

3 Setting Up Fixtures, Mannequins, and Props: Bringing Your Display to Life

Now comes the fun part—**building your window!** But it's not just about placing items randomly. **Every element should serve a purpose** in guiding the customer's eye toward what matters most.

◆ Fixtures & Stands: The Backbone of Your Display

Using different heights and structures **adds depth and movement**:
✔ **Pedestals & platforms** – Elevate key items for prominence.
✔ **Racks & shelving** – Organize and create layers.
✔ **Suspended elements** – Floating items add **whimsy and curiosity**.

☛ Example: A jewelry store might use **glass cubes** at varying heights to showcase **rings, necklaces, and bracelets separately**, creating a **luxurious feel**.

◆ Mannequins: Telling a Story Without Words

A **static mannequin is boring**—give it **life and personality!**
✔ **Pose them naturally** – Walking, reaching, or interacting.
✔ **Group them dynamically** – Create a sense of movement.
✔ **Accessorize fully** – Show the **complete look** to inspire buyers.

☛ Example: A **sportswear shop** could pose a **mannequin mid-sprint** in running gear to show **action and energy**, rather than just standing still.

◆ Props: Setting the Scene

Props add **context and storytelling** to your display. Use them wisely:
✔ **Seasonal props** – Leaves for autumn, fairy lights for Christmas.
✔ **Brand-related elements** – If you sell books, an open book display adds charm.
✔ **Lifestyle hints** – A cozy chair with a coffee cup in a clothing store suggests *relaxed weekend vibes*.

👉 Example: A **bakery window** could feature **fake flour dusting, rolling pins, and wooden crates** to make customers feel like they've stepped into a **rustic kitchen**.

💡 **Pro Tip:** Avoid **clutter**—props should **enhance, not overpower** the products.

4 Adjusting for Different Window Sizes: Big or Small, Make It Work

Not all window spaces are **big and luxurious**—some are **tiny or oddly shaped**. But great displays **work at any scale** if designed correctly.

◆ For Large Windows: Go Bold & Layered

✔ Use **large-scale props and focal points** to avoid an empty feel.
✔ Create **depth** by placing products in the **foreground, midground, and background**.
✔ Introduce **movement elements** (rotating stands, hanging signs) to make use of space.

👉 Example: A **department store** can create a **life-sized winter village scene** with mannequins as **ice skaters and skiers**.

◆ For Small Windows: Focus & Simplify

✔ Use **fewer items**—small spaces get cluttered quickly.
✔ Stick to **one strong focal point** (e.g., a single mannequin in an eye-catching outfit).
✔ Use **mirrors to create the illusion of space**.

👉 Example: A **jewelry shop with a small window** could use a **single, elegant necklace on a velvet bust** with **a soft spotlight** for **maximum impact**.

💡 **Pro Tip:** If your **window is oddly shaped**, use **floating shelves, wall decals, or hanging elements** to work with the space.

From Plan to Reality

Setting up a **successful window display** is both **an art and a science**. By following these **practical steps**, you can create **an engaging, visually stunning display** that **captures attention and increases foot traffic**.

- **Plan your layout carefully** – Sketch it out before starting.
- **Choose the right products** – Feature bestsellers and seasonally relevant items.
- **Use props, mannequins, and fixtures** to **tell a story**.
- **Adjust based on window size** – Large displays need depth, small ones need focus.

A great display doesn't just **showcase products**—it **creates a moment, an experience, and a reason for people to stop, look, and walk in.**

Maximizing Engagement and Foot Traffic: Turning Passersby into Paying Customers

A beautifully designed window display isn't just about looking good—it's about **grabbing attention, sparking curiosity, and driving people into your store**. But with so many distractions on the high street or in a shopping mall, how do you **cut through the noise** and make your display truly **irresistible**?

---

1 Using Movement and Lighting to Attract Customers

💡 **Why it Matters:**
Human eyes are naturally drawn to **light, motion, and contrast**. A **static display** might look beautiful, but a **dynamic one** stops people in their tracks.

* **Lighting: Setting the Mood & Drawing Attention**

Lighting isn't just about visibility—it influences **mood, perception, and buying decisions**.

✔ **Spotlights & Directional Lighting** – Highlight key products and create **visual hierarchy**.
✔ **Colored Lighting** – Different colors evoke different emotions (e.g., **warm tones** feel inviting, while **cool tones** feel luxurious and modern).
✔ **Backlighting & Neon Accents** – Add a **glow effect** for a futuristic or high-end look.
✔ **Timed Lighting Sequences** – Shift colors or intensity throughout the day for a **dynamic feel**.

👉 **Example:** A **high-end watch retailer** might use **focused, warm lighting** to create a feeling of **exclusivity and sophistication**, while a **sportswear store** could use **bright, high-contrast lighting** for an **energetic and bold look**.

✦ Movement: The Power of Kinetic Displays

Motion grabs attention **instantly**. Instead of a **static setup**, introduce **movement**:

✔️ **Rotating platforms** – Showcase a featured product from all angles.
✔️ **Hanging mobiles** – Gently swaying elements add a mesmerizing effect.
✔️ **Digital screens** – Play short, looping videos or interactive content.
✔️ **Mechanical displays** – Think of department store holiday windows with **animated figures**.

👉 **Example:** A **toy store** could feature a **moving train set**, drawing kids (and their parents) inside, while a **tech store** might have a **rotating 3D hologram** of a new product.

💡 **Pro Tip:** Even small, **subtle movement** (like flickering LED lights or a slow-turning platform) can make a **huge difference** in catching someone's eye.

2 Creating Instagrammable Displays: Making Your Store a Social Media Magnet

📍 Why it Matters:
In the age of **Instagram, TikTok, and Snapchat**, your shop window isn't just **a display**—it's an opportunity for **free advertising**. If people love it, they'll snap a photo, **share it online**, and bring more foot traffic your way.

• How to Make Your Display Insta-Worthy

✔️ **Big, Bold, & Unique Elements** – Giant props, striking backdrops, or neon signs work wonders.
✔️ **Interactive Features** – Mirrors, cut-out frames, or AR (Augmented Reality) experiences.
✔️ **Witty or Inspirational Text** – Add a **catchy phrase** that makes people stop and take a pic (e.g., *"Shop Till You Drop! 🛍️"*).
✔️ **Brand Hashtags & QR Codes** – Encourage customers to **tag your store** and scan for discounts.

👉 **Example:** A **florist** could create a **living flower wall**, while a **fashion boutique** might have a **neon sign saying, "You Look Amazing"** in front of a stylish backdrop.

📍 Pro Tip: If customers **share** their photos, **reshare them on your store's social media**—this builds a sense of **community and FOMO (fear of missing out)**.

③ Cross-Selling and Upselling Through Visual Merchandising

💡 Why it Matters:
A great display doesn't just **sell one product**—it **influences multiple purchases**. Done right, visual merchandising can **increase basket size** and **boost revenue per customer**.

◆ Cross-Selling: Suggesting Complementary Products

Showcase items that **naturally go together** to encourage customers to buy more.

✔ **Fashion Retail** – If you're displaying a stunning dress, add matching shoes and accessories nearby.
✔ **Tech Stores** – Pair a laptop with a stylish carrying case and wireless mouse.
✔ **Grocery & Food** – A wine shop might feature **cheese and crackers alongside bottles**.

👉 **Example:** A **men's clothing store** could style a mannequin with **a full outfit**—blazer, shirt, trousers, and shoes—so customers see the **entire look, not just one item**.

◆ Upselling: Encouraging Higher-Value Purchases

Make premium products **stand out** in your display by:

✔ **Using prime spots** – Place **higher-ticket items** at **eye level**.
✔ **Creating a comparison** – Show a **basic version** next to the **deluxe edition**.
✔ **Adding "best-seller" or "limited edition" labels** – Create urgency.

👉 **Example:** A **cosmetics store** might highlight a **luxury perfume** in a **glass display case**, emphasizing its **premium status**.

💡 **Pro Tip:** The **more seamlessly** you integrate complementary products into your display, the **more natural** the upsell will feel.

4 Measuring the Success of Your Displays: What Works & What Doesn't?

Why it Matters:
A window display might look **stunning**, but if it doesn't **drive sales**, it's just decoration. Tracking **key performance metrics** helps you **fine-tune your approach** and create **displays that convert**.

Key Metrics to Track

✔ **Foot Traffic Increase** – Are more people walking into your store after changing the display?

✔ **Sales Uplift** – Did featured products sell better than usual?

✔ **Dwell Time** – Are people stopping to look, or just walking past?

✔ **Social Media Engagement** – Are people taking photos and tagging your store?

✔ **QR Code Scans & Online Conversions** – If you use digital integration, are people engaging?

How to Collect Data

✔ **Use Door Counters** – Track how many people enter before vs. after a new display.

✔ **Train Staff to Observe & Engage** – Ask customers what caught their attention.

✔ **Check Sales Reports** – Compare product performance before and after a display update.

✔ **Monitor Social Media Mentions** – Are people talking about your display online?

👉 **Example:** If a **summer-themed display featuring sunglasses and beach hats** results in a **20% increase in sales for those items**, you know your concept worked!

Pro Tip: If something **isn't working**, don't be afraid to **tweak and test**—small changes (like adjusting lighting or layout) can have **big impacts**.

Turning Window Browsers into Buyers

A great display **doesn't just showcase products—it creates an experience, tells a story, and emotionally connects with shoppers.** By incorporating **lighting, movement, social media integration, and smart merchandising techniques**, you can turn **your shop window into a powerful, revenue-driving tool**.

Quick Recap:
- Use **lighting and movement** to draw attention.
- Create **Instagrammable displays** for **free social media exposure**.
- Maximize sales with **cross-selling and upselling strategies**.
- **Track and measure** what works—and keep improving.

Budget-Friendly Window Dressing Tips: Stunning Displays on a Shoestring Budget

Creating an eye-catching, effective window display doesn't have to **break the bank**. In fact, some of the most **memorable displays** are made with **creativity, resourcefulness**, and a little **DIY spirit**. Whether you're just starting out or looking to keep your costs down, these budget-friendly tips will show you how to make the most of your resources without sacrificing impact.

---

1 DIY Display Hacks: Transforming Everyday Items into Visual Masterpieces

💡 **Why it Matters:**
The beauty of DIY displays is that **creativity** is your **most valuable resource**. With a bit of time and effort, you can turn **ordinary objects** into **extraordinary window displays**.

◆ Use Repurposed Materials

Old materials are often more **durable and unique** than new ones! Look around your store or home for **unused items** that can be repurposed:

✔ **Wooden pallets** – Stack them to create platforms or shelves. They make for great **rustic displays**.
✔ **Old frames** – Repurpose picture frames for signage or create **artistic backgrounds**.
✔ **Scrap fabric** – Turn scrap fabric into **banners, drapes**, or **backdrops**.

✔ **Cardboard boxes** – With a little paint or decoration, they can be used to create **stylized stands** or **thematic elements**.

👉 **Example:** If you're creating a **vintage-inspired display**, you could repurpose old **suitcases** to create a **stacked, travel-themed focal point**.

◆ Get Crafty with Paper

Paper is **inexpensive** and **versatile**. Create **paper flowers**, **origami figures**, or **folded paper backdrops** to bring a unique touch to your display.

✔ **Paper Bunting & Garlands** – Use colored or patterned paper to create hanging decorations.
✔ **DIY Paper Flowers** – Turn simple tissue paper or old books into **eye-catching floral displays**.
✔ **Paper Mâché Objects** – Make lightweight yet durable props using newspaper and glue.

👉 **Example:** A **flower shop** could create a **garden-like feel** by making **oversized paper flowers** to display in their window.

◆ Repurpose Old Fixtures and Furniture

Don't throw out that **old shelving unit** or **cluttered drawer**—they can become the perfect fixture for your window.

✔ **Turn old bookshelves into display racks** for clothing or accessories.
✔ **Repurpose crates or wooden boxes** for a **stackable display** to hold products.
✔ **Use old mirrors** to make a **dramatic backdrop** or even **reflect light** onto key products.

👉 **Example:** If you're in the **home décor business**, an **old ladder** can be used as a charming display rack for rustic throws, pillows, or art prints.

💡 **Pro Tip:** The **DIY approach** not only saves money but adds a personal, **one-of-a-kind feel** to your window, making your display stand out in a crowd.

---

2 Upcycling and Repurposing Materials: Giving Old Items New Life

💡 **Why it Matters:**
Upcycling is the art of turning **old, unused items** into something **new and useful**, and it's a fantastic way to create unique window displays on a budget. Not only is it good for your **wallet**, but it's also great for the **environment**—a win-win!

◆ Furniture and Home Décor Upcycle

Old or broken furniture doesn't need to be thrown out. With a little creativity, it can become **the focal point** of your display.

✔️ **Old chairs** – Turn them into a **stylized product display** by adding shelving or hanging accessories from the chair's backrest.
✔️ **Repurpose an old door** – Use a **vintage door** as a backdrop for your display. You could paint it, add hooks, or turn it into a **frame** for a larger visual.
✔️ **Upcycled furniture** – Use **dresser drawers** or **old cabinets** to create **distinct display sections**.

👉 **Example:** A **home goods store** could use a **reclaimed wooden door** as a backdrop for showcasing vintage, artisan kitchenware.

◆ Fabric & Textile Repurposing

Old textiles are not only **inexpensive**, but they can be transformed into **creative, high-impact displays**.

✔️ **Vintage tablecloths or old bed sheets** – Turn these into **backdrops, drapes, or canopies**.

✔ **Old sweaters or scarves** – Repurpose them into **product display coverings** or even create **wall hangings**.
✔ **T-shirts** – Use shirts with interesting patterns or logos to create **cushions, banners**, or even **covering displays**.

👉 **Example:** A **vintage clothing store** could use **old denim** or **flannel shirts** to create **fabrics and textures** that emphasize the store's **retro vibe**.

---

③ Collaborating with Local Artists and Businesses: Building Community Connections

🔔 **Why it Matters:**
You don't have to do everything **alone**. By collaborating with **local artists, crafters**, and **businesses**, you can create **dynamic, budget-friendly displays** while also strengthening ties within your **local community**.

◆ Work with Local Artists for Unique Touches

Many artists or designers are happy to **collaborate** on displays in exchange for **exposure** or a **small fee**. You can even consider allowing them to sell their work within your store.

✔ **Custom Artworks** – Have a local artist paint a mural or create a custom piece for your display.
✔ **Handcrafted Props** – Collaborate with a local woodworker or sculptor to make unique props.
✔ **Installations** – Invite an artist to create a **temporary installation** in your window, such as a **pop-up exhibit**.

👉 **Example:** A **bookshop** might partner with a local artist to create an **interactive window display** of **hand-painted books** or **literary sculptures**.

◆ Partner with Other Small Businesses

If your business is part of a **local shopping district**, consider **cross-promoting** with neighboring stores to create a **unified window display**.

✔ **Collaborative Themes** – Team up with a nearby **coffee shop** and feature their drinks alongside your pastries or retail products.

✔ **Co-Branding Displays** – Share space and resources to create a **larger, more impactful display** that highlights the strengths of each business.

✔ **Co-Host Events** – Partner with another shop to **host events** or **themed displays** that can attract customers for both businesses.

👉 **Example:** A **flower shop** and a **local café** might combine their products in a **seasonal display** featuring **fresh flowers** and **signature coffee mugs**, drawing more traffic to both.

Creativity Over Cost

Window dressing on a budget doesn't mean you have to sacrifice style or creativity. By embracing **DIY solutions, upcycling materials**, and **collaborating with local artists and businesses**, you can create **unique, high-impact displays** that will **grab attention**, increase **foot traffic**, and make a **lasting impression**—all without spending a fortune.

💡 **Quick Recap:**
- Get creative with **DIY hacks** and **upcycled materials**.
- Work with **local artists** to add **personalized, unique touches** to your displays.
- Collaborate with **neighboring businesses** to create **shared, community-driven themes**.

Common Mistakes and How to Avoid Them: Keep Your Displays Clean, Effective, and Engaging

Creating a **captivating window display** takes skill, but even the best designers make mistakes. Whether you're a seasoned pro or just starting out, it's easy to fall into common pitfalls. However, by being aware of these missteps, you can ensure your displays always shine and leave a lasting impression.

---

1 Overloading the Display with Too Many Elements

💡 Why It's a Mistake:
When it comes to **window dressing, less is often more**. It's tempting to showcase as many products as possible or pack in numerous visual elements to grab attention. However, an overcrowded display can overwhelm your audience and diminish the impact of the **key products** you're trying to highlight.

◆ Why Overloading Hurts

A cluttered window display can confuse shoppers, making it difficult for them to focus on anything specific. When there's too much going on, customers may not know where to look first, and important items could be **lost in the noise**. Instead of creating a **strong first impression**, you risk **distracting** potential customers with **visual chaos**.

◆ How to Avoid It

- **Focus on Key Products**: Instead of trying to display everything in your store, choose one or two **hero products** to highlight. Make these items the **focal point** of your display to draw attention.

- **Embrace White Space**: Giving your display some **breathing room** allows the viewer's eyes to naturally wander from one element to the next. White space helps highlight your main products and prevents the display from feeling overcrowded.

- **Use Layers, Not Clutter**: If you want to include a variety of products, think in terms of **layering**. Create depth and focus by placing larger items in the background and smaller items in the foreground. This way, your display feels dynamic without becoming chaotic.

☞ **Example:** A **fashion boutique** may choose to showcase **one statement piece of clothing**, like a dress, and accent it with **minimal accessories**, such as a stylish handbag and shoes. This gives the display focus and clarity without overwhelming the viewer.

---

②Ignoring Sightlines and Customer Flow

💡 Why It's a Mistake:
Sightlines refer to how customers **see and engage with your display** from different vantage points. If your window is blocked by obstructions or your products are positioned at **odd angles**, customers may not be able to view your display clearly. Similarly, how a shopper moves around your store and approaches the window can greatly influence their perception and engagement with the products.

◆ Why Sightlines Matter

Shoppers often make quick decisions based on what they see first. If your window is designed in such a way that potential customers **can't see** your best items or if the **flow of the display** isn't intuitive, you may miss the opportunity to catch their attention.

◆ How to Avoid It

- **Plan Your Display from All Angles**: Walk around your store and see your display from different viewpoints. If something is obstructed or hard to see, it needs to be adjusted.

- **Keep Products at Eye Level**: Shoppers are most likely to engage with products at **eye level**, so make sure your **best-selling or most visually striking products** are positioned there.

- **Consider Customer Movement**: How do you want customers to interact with your window? Is it meant to **lure them inside**? Make sure the display invites people to **move toward** it or encourages them to step into the store for a closer look. Your display should follow a **natural flow** to guide the customer's attention and actions.

👉 **Example:** In a **toy store**, placing **brightly colored toys** at the front of the window and ensuring the display flows from left to right can entice parents and children to **step in** and engage with the toys directly.

③ Failing to Update Displays Regularly

💡 Why It's a Mistake:

One of the most damaging mistakes you can make is **leaving the same window display up for too long**. After a certain point, displays can start to feel **stale** or **uninspiring**, and customers may overlook them. A **static display** doesn't offer much incentive for return visits, and it may make your store seem **out of touch** with trends or seasons.

◆ Why Regular Updates Matter

Freshness is key in window dressing. Customers are more likely to engage with a display that feels **new, exciting**, and **relevant** to the current season, trend, or promotion. Failing to update regularly can also create the perception that your store is **unresponsive to change**, which could deter shoppers from entering or returning.

◆ How to Avoid It

- **Set a Schedule**: Make it a habit to update your window displays regularly—ideally every **2-4 weeks**, depending on the season, sales cycles, or promotions.

- **Use Seasonal Themes**: Plan your displays around upcoming holidays, seasons, or events. This gives you natural opportunities to refresh your look and engage customers with timely, relevant content.

- **Rotate Featured Products**: Even if you have a popular product, rotating its position in the window or updating its props can **revitalize its appeal** and maintain customer interest.

👉 **Example:** A **skincare store** might feature **new arrivals or seasonal products** during certain months, such as **summer SPF products** in May and **holiday gift sets** in December. Regularly updating these displays ensures they stay **relevant** and **exciting** for return customers.

Stay Mindful, Keep It Simple, and Keep It Fresh

Effective window dressing is about more than just **showing off products**—it's about **crafting a visual story** that draws people in and keeps them engaged. By avoiding common mistakes like **overloading your display, ignoring sightlines**, and **failing to update regularly**, you can create displays that not only capture attention but also **generate foot traffic** and **boost sales**.

💡 **Key Takeaways**:
- **Keep it simple**: Avoid overcrowding and focus on your key products.
- **Consider sightlines**: Ensure products are positioned for maximum visibility and flow.
- **Update regularly**: Keep your displays fresh and relevant to maintain excitement.

The Difference Between Male and Female Targeted Window Dressing Displays

When it comes to window dressing, one of the most significant factors in designing a display is understanding your **target audience**. Gender plays a crucial role in influencing how customers perceive and interact with your store's offerings. Whether you're dressing a display for **male** or **female** consumers, the approach, messaging, and visual appeal should be tailored to each audience's unique preferences, behaviors, and psychological triggers.

Why Gender-Specific Displays Matter

In retail, it's essential to recognize that **males** and **females** often have different shopping behaviors, preferences, and visual sensitivities. While generalizations can sometimes oversimplify these differences, studies and consumer insights show that gender-targeted window displays can **boost engagement** and **increase sales** by speaking directly to each group's interests, lifestyle, and aspirations. **Tailoring** your window displays helps create a **connection** that draws customers in and makes them feel understood.

---

1 Male-Targeted Window Dressing Displays

Key Characteristics of Male Shoppers:

Functional over Decorative: Male consumers tend to prioritize **functionality** over aesthetic appeal. They often look for **products that solve a problem** or serve a **specific purpose**.

Minimalism and Clean Lines: Males are generally drawn to clean, uncluttered displays with **clear product emphasis**. Overly ornate or overly busy designs can be off-putting.

Bold and Simple Messaging: Men often respond well to straightforward messaging that conveys **utility**, **performance**, and **value**.

Subtle Color Palettes: While bold and dark colors like **blues**, **grays**, and **blacks** are popular with male shoppers, **neutral tones** or **earthy shades** can also work effectively, evoking a sense of **strength**, **stability**, and **practicality**.

Effective Design Techniques for Male Displays

- **Highlight Product Features**: For male-targeted displays, show off the **key features** of products. Use signage that emphasizes **quality**, **innovation**, and **functionality**. For example, a **sporting goods** store might focus on high-performance gear with a prominent sign that says, "**Engineered for Peak Performance.**"

- **Minimalist Approach**: Stick to **clean lines** and **simple layouts** that highlight your product without excessive decoration. For instance, in a **tech store**, a **sleek, minimalist display** of the latest gadgets or tools, placed on floating shelves or pedestals, will communicate sophistication and focus on the product's **functionality**.

- **Masculine Props**: Use **industrial props** like metal stands, leather cushions, or wooden crates to enhance a sense of **ruggedness**. Avoid over-decorating with frivolous items; instead, choose props that emphasize **strength** or **reliability**—like a **steel toolbox** for a DIY store or a **weathered jacket** in an outdoor apparel shop.

👉 **Example**: A **watch store** targeting men may feature a **sleek black watch** front and center, surrounded by minimalistic **dark-toned shelves** with a **single spotlight**. The display could include a small, simple sign reading, "Built for Durability," which emphasizes the **rugged** and **practical** nature of the product.

---

② Female-Targeted Window Dressing Displays

Key Characteristics of Female Shoppers:

- **Emotion-Driven Shopping**: Female shoppers are often drawn to displays that evoke an emotional response, whether it's through **style**, **aesthetic appeal**, or the **story** behind the product.

- **Decorative and Detailed**: Women tend to appreciate displays with **more intricate details**, soft textures, and **decorative accents** that appeal to the senses.

- **Social and Aspirational Messaging**: Women are more likely to respond to **social or aspirational messages** that promise a lifestyle enhancement or **self-expression**.

- **Vibrant and Warm Colors**: Female-targeted displays are often brighter and more vibrant, with colors like **pinks**, **purples**, **pastels**, and **rich jewel tones** that evoke **warmth**, **creativity**, and **nurturing**.

Effective Design Techniques for Female Displays

- **Aesthetic Appeal and Styling**: For female-targeted displays, embrace **soft textures** like fabrics, florals, and gentle curves. For example, in a **fashion store**, a **mannequin** wearing a **chic, floral dress** could be surrounded by **elegant props** like a **vintage suitcase** or a **delicate mirror**.

- **Emotional Connection**: Use **color psychology** and **symbols of luxury** or **elegance** to convey a **sense of empowerment** or indulgence. For example, a **high-end cosmetics brand** could emphasize femininity with rich **gold accents** and a **soft pink** backdrop, making it feel indulgent and personal.

- **Dynamic, Storytelling Displays**: Women are often more drawn to displays that **tell a story**. For example, a **jewelry store** might use a display where pieces are arranged in the context of a **romantic or celebratory theme**, such as **engagement rings** paired with **flowers** or **love notes**, which immediately creates an emotional response.

👉 **Example**: A **women's boutique** might showcase a **bohemian summer dress** as the centerpiece, surrounded by **soft, pastel-colored scarves, delicate jewelry**, and **natural wood props** like **driftwood** or **succulent plants**. The color palette could include **muted pinks, creams**, and **earthy tones**, appealing to the consumer's desire for **comfort** and **style**.

---

3 Gender-Neutral and Inclusive Displays

In today's diverse and inclusive marketplace, there's a growing trend toward **gender-neutral displays** that appeal to all customers. These displays blend elements from both male and female-targeted strategies to create a balanced, inclusive atmosphere that resonates with a wider audience.

Use of Neutral Colors: Neutral tones like **grays**, **whites**, and **black**, paired with occasional pops of **bold colors**, can attract both male and female customers without leaning too heavily in either direction.
Universal Design Elements: Displays can focus on universally appealing values like **quality**, **simplicity**, and **timelessness**, which resonate with a broader demographic. For instance, a **minimalist fashion store** could feature high-quality, versatile **clothing** that appeals equally to all genders, showcased with **sleek, monochrome displays** and subtle, stylish props.

Key Takeaways for Gender-Specific Window Dressing

Male-targeted displays should be **functional, minimal**, and **straightforward**, with a focus on **quality** and **utility**.
Female-targeted displays should embrace **emotion, aesthetic appeal**, and **storytelling**, with an emphasis on **style, luxury**, and **personal expression**.
Gender-neutral displays use a **balanced** design approach, incorporating **universal appeal** and **timeless style** for a broad demographic.

By understanding these nuanced differences and tailoring your approach, you can ensure your window displays speak directly to the interests and preferences of your target customers—whether male, female, or everyone in between.

Future Trends in Shop Displays

As the retail landscape evolves, so do the ways in which stores engage with customers through their window displays. The future of shop displays promises to be **innovative, interactive,** and **sustainable**. Retailers are increasingly focusing on creating experiences that **delight, inspire,** and **resonate** with customers, pushing the boundaries of traditional window dressing. Here are three key trends shaping the future of shop displays: **sustainability, digitalization,** and **personalization**.

1 Sustainable and Eco-Friendly Window Dressing

As consumers become more conscious of the environment, there's a growing demand for **sustainable practices** across all industries, including retail. **Eco-friendly window displays** are not just a trend—they represent a fundamental shift in how retailers approach **product display** and **design aesthetics**. By adopting sustainable strategies, shops can attract eco-conscious customers and reduce their environmental footprint.

Why Sustainability Matters

- **Ethical Consumerism**: Shoppers today are more likely to support brands that align with their **values**. Sustainable displays show a commitment to the environment, which can improve customer loyalty and boost brand reputation.

- **Waste Reduction**: Traditional window displays often involve temporary materials like plastic, paper, and other non-recyclable items. As **sustainability** becomes a priority, retailers are moving towards **recyclable, biodegradable,** and **upcycled materials** in their displays.

Sustainable Design Techniques

- **Recycled Materials**: Using **recycled wood**, **metal**, or **glass** to create sleek and stylish display fixtures. This helps minimize waste while giving the display a modern, eco-conscious edge.

- **Minimal Waste**: Reducing the number of disposable items used in window displays. Instead, opt for reusable structures or **modular displays** that can be reconfigured for multiple seasons.

- **Eco-Friendly Signage**: Use **water-based paints** or **plant-based inks** for banners and labels. Sustainable **fabric signage** and **hanging materials** can replace plastic alternatives, while also adding texture and charm to the display.

- **Repurposed Items**: Embrace **upcycling** by turning old products into display props. For example, **upcycled furniture** or **old packaging** can be transformed into creative stand-alone pieces that tell a story of sustainability.

👉 **Example**: A **clothing store** could create a window display entirely from **recycled denim** to showcase its new collection. By incorporating **repurposed mannequins**, **eco-friendly fabrics**, and **upcycled shelving**, the store would emphasize both style and sustainability in a visually appealing and environmentally responsible way.

---

2 The Rise of Digital and Interactive Displays

As the digital age continues to unfold, **technology** is playing an increasingly important role in shaping how retailers engage with customers. **Interactive digital displays** are revolutionizing window dressing, allowing stores to create **immersive experiences** that capture attention and drive foot traffic.

Why Digital and Interactive Displays Matter

- **Engagement and Interactivity**: Static window displays are being replaced by **dynamic, interactive screens** that engage customers in new ways. These displays not only capture attention but also encourage customers to **participate** in the display experience.

- **Real-Time Updates**: Digital displays allow for **easy updates** and **real-time changes**, making it simpler for retailers to showcase new products or adjust for changing trends without having to redo the entire display.

- **Increased Consumer Involvement**: Interactive features, like **touchscreens** or **motion-sensing technology**, enable customers to interact with products, view product details, or even **customize items** right from the display.

Types of Digital and Interactive Displays

- **Touchscreen Displays**: Customers can tap on the screen to learn more about products, watch demo videos, or explore product features. This is particularly popular in **tech** and **beauty stores**, where product knowledge is key.

- **Augmented Reality (AR)**: Imagine a **clothing store** where customers can see themselves trying on outfits virtually through AR technology embedded in the window display. This creates a fun, engaging experience and encourages customers to step inside the store.

- **QR Code Integration**: Integrating **QR codes** into window displays allows passersby to scan them with their phones and access exclusive discounts, more product info, or a **virtual shopping experience**.

- **Projection Mapping**: **Projection mapping** is the art of projecting images onto surfaces to create a dynamic 3D experience. This technology allows brands to create immersive, high-energy window displays that can change throughout the day, attracting different crowds at different times.

👉 **Example**: A **high-end electronics store** might showcase the latest gadgets in its window using **interactive touchscreens** where customers can swipe through product features and demos. These displays could also offer **exclusive virtual tours** of new tech releases, creating an unforgettable shopping experience even before customers walk through the door.

---

3 AI and Personalization in Retail Spaces

The future of window displays is not just about captivating visuals—it's also about **personalizing the shopping experience**. Thanks to advancements in **artificial intelligence (AI)**, retailers now have the ability to tailor their displays to the **preferences** and **behaviors** of individual customers, creating a much more **targeted** and **relevant** experience.

Why AI and Personalization Matter

- **Customer-Centric Approach**: Personalization enables retailers to cater to specific tastes and needs, making customers feel like the store truly understands them and their desires.

- **Increased Conversion Rates**: Personalized displays can **boost sales** by highlighting products that are most relevant to a customer's preferences or **shopping history**. AI can help analyze data and suggest products that might resonate with different customer segments.

- **Data-Driven Insights**: AI tools enable retailers to collect valuable data on how customers interact with their displays. This insight allows for **more strategic decisions** regarding product placements, messaging, and promotions.

AI and Personalization Techniques

- **Smart Displays**: With AI-powered sensors, **smart window displays** can detect when someone is passing by and adjust the content based on the person's **demographics** (age, gender, etc.), previous interactions, or even **weather patterns**.

- **Product Recommendations**: Based on **real-time data**, a digital display could suggest products that match the customer's past preferences or purchases, creating a seamless shopping experience.

- **Dynamic Content**: Personalized messaging, tailored offers, and product recommendations can be adjusted automatically based on customer behavior, making each window display feel unique and relevant to every individual who sees it.

👉 **Example**: A **beauty retailer** could install an **AI-driven digital mirror** in the store window that detects customers' facial features and recommends skincare products or makeup shades tailored to their skin tone. The AI could offer **personalized suggestions**, making the experience feel intimate and targeted.

Key Takeaways:

- **Sustainable and Eco-Friendly Window Dressing**: Consumers are increasingly seeking brands that align with their eco-conscious values. Use recyclable materials, upcycled items, and minimal waste strategies to create a **sustainable** shopping experience.

- **Digital and Interactive Displays**: The future of window dressing includes **interactive technology** like touchscreens, AR, and projection mapping to **engage** and **immerse** customers in dynamic shopping experiences.

- **AI and Personalization**: The integration of **AI** allows retailers to create **customized, data-driven** window displays that cater to individual consumer preferences, increasing engagement and **conversion rates**.

As technology advances and consumer behaviors continue to shift, the possibilities for **innovative window displays** are endless. By embracing **sustainability, digital interactivity**, and **personalization**, you can stay ahead of the curve and create a **cutting-edge retail experience** that will captivate customers for years to come.

Conclusion: Final Thoughts on Creativity and Strategy

Window dressing and shop displays are not just about aesthetics—they are powerful tools that can drive consumer behavior, enhance brand perception, and boost sales. In the ever-evolving world of retail, **creativity** and **strategy** are essential to creating displays that stand out and leave a lasting impression.

The Intersection of Creativity and Strategy

At the heart of every successful window display is a **fusion of creativity and strategy**. Creativity fuels the **visual appeal**, while strategy ensures that the display serves a **purpose** beyond decoration—whether that's to **tell a story**, **highlight a product**, or **evoke an emotion**. When these two elements align, the result is a window display that **captures attention**, **engages the audience**, and **inspires action**.

The Role of Creativity

Creativity allows you to take risks, break the mold, and think outside the box. It's about experimenting with **new materials**, embracing **bold colors**, or incorporating **unexpected elements** into your display. Creativity also fuels **innovation**—whether through unique **concepts** or incorporating **cutting-edge technology** like digital displays or interactive features. The goal is to create an experience that's not just visually captivating but also **memorable**, so customers are compelled to return.

The Role of Strategy

While creativity drives the **artistic vision**, strategy ensures that your window displays have a **clear objective**. Every element in your display should serve a purpose. Whether it's **boosting foot traffic**, **showcasing**

a new collection, or **reinforcing brand values**, a well-planned display strategically **guides customers** toward making a purchase. This means understanding your target audience, leveraging **psychological principles**, and aligning your displays with the broader goals of your business.

The Power of Storytelling in Displays

One of the most powerful strategies in window dressing is **storytelling**. When a window display tells a compelling story, it draws customers in and creates an emotional connection. Whether you're crafting a **seasonal narrative**, **showcasing a product's journey**, or highlighting **brand values**, the story behind your display can turn a simple product showcase into an **experience**.

Crafting a Narrative

The story could be as simple as illustrating the **craftsmanship** behind a product or as elaborate as creating a **fantastical scene** that transports customers to a different world. A well-told story not only captures attention but also encourages customers to interact with your display, either by physically entering the store or engaging with your brand in other ways.

Adapting to Change

Retail is a constantly shifting environment, and successful window displays are those that can **adapt to changes** in trends, seasons, and consumer behavior. Keeping your displays **fresh** and **relevant** is crucial in maintaining customer interest and encouraging repeat visits. Be prepared to update your windows regularly, not just for the sake of novelty, but to stay **aligned** with **market demands, seasonal shifts,** and **customer expectations.**

Embrace Change

Incorporating **seasonal themes, current trends,** and **emerging technologies** into your displays helps keep your store's image **dynamic.** Don't be afraid to experiment, fail, and try again. **Innovation** often comes from pushing the boundaries of what's been done before, and **adaptability** is key to staying relevant in a fast-paced retail landscape.

The Long-Term Impact

At its core, effective window dressing is about **creating connections.** When customers are drawn into your store by a **compelling display,** they're more likely to feel a deeper connection to your brand, resulting in both immediate sales and long-term loyalty. Whether it's a **memorable shopping experience,** a **creative display** that sparks conversation, or an **interactive moment** that engages their curiosity, a well-executed window display has the potential to transform a **first-time visitor** into a **regular customer.**

Brand Identity

Window displays are also an extension of your brand's **identity.** They communicate who you are, what you stand for, and what your products represent. Consistency across all your displays, whether in-store or through windows, reinforces your brand's **message** and ensures that customers have a cohesive and recognizable experience every time they interact with your store.

In Closing: A Balanced Approach

The future of window dressing lies in a **balanced approach**—one that combines the **artistic freedom** of creativity with the **purposeful intent** of strategy. Retailers who master this balance will not only craft visually stunning displays but will also create powerful, lasting connections with their customers. It's about more than just showcasing products; it's about creating an experience that **informs**, **inspires**, and **engages**.

So, as you step into the world of window dressing, remember: every display is an opportunity to **tell a story**, to **connect with customers**, and to **reinforce your brand**. With a **thoughtful approach**, **creative vision**, and **strategic intent**, your window displays will not only **capture attention** but will also **drive results**.

Chris

Printed in Dunstable, United Kingdom

73792641R00040